"Daily gratitude is the key to a ha...

Every Day
Thankful

365
Blessings, Graces and Gratitudes

Becca Anderson

Foreword by Nina Lesowitz, author of *Living Life as a Thank You*

Design: Laura Mejía

For permission requests, please contact the publisher at:
Mango Publishing Group
2850 Douglas Road, 3rd Floor
Coral Gables, FL 33134 USA
info@mango.bz

For special orders, quantity sales, course adoptions and corporate sales, please email the publisher at sales@mango.bz.

For trade and wholesale sales, please contact Ingram Publisher Services at customer.service@ingramcontent.com or +1.800.509.4887.

Every Day Thankful: 365 Blessings, Graces and Gratitudes
ISBN: 978-1-63353-527-5
Printed in the United States of America

Deepest love and appreciation to the elders in my family who survived the Great Depression and shared stories of living through hard times with humility and a sense of gratitude. I owe you so much for the wisdom.

Wake at dawn with a winged
Heart and give thanks for
Another day of loving.

—Khalil Gibran

Table of Contents

Foreword

The Importance of Living Life as a Thank You
by Nina Lesowitz

Are you tired of walking around with a hole in your heart? Do you need more inspiration? Studies show—and experts counsel—that gratitude is a key component of our own happiness. People who are grateful about events and experiences from the past, who celebrate the triumphs instead of focusing on the losses or disappointments, tend to be more satisfied in the present. In her popular book The Secret, Rhonda Byrne writes, "With all that I have read and all that I have experienced in my own life using The Secret, the power of gratitude stands above everything else. If you do only one thing with the knowledge of this book, use gratitude until it becomes your way of life."

The recent buzz surrounding the power of gratitude is overwhelmingly positive. Jeffery Zaslow, a columnist for the Wall Street Journal, recently wrote there may be a positive by-product of the troubled economic times that followed the 2008 stock market dive: a decrease in the urge to complain. "People who still have jobs are finding reasons to be appreciative. It feels unseemly to complain about not getting a raise when your neighbor is unemployed," he wrote. "Homeowners are unhappy that home values have fallen, but it's a relief to avoid foreclosure."

Indeed, in these times of economic woe, gratitude is popping up everywhere. Turn on the TV. We listened as a career coach on The Today Show advised job seekers to put the words "thank you" in their job search tool kits, declaring that the key to distinguishing oneself from the masses is to send a thank you note. Click on to Facebook and check out the gratitude groups, where hundreds of people log on each day to give thanks for everything from the sun rising that morning to their neighborhood dog parks. Cathy, of Greenville, South Carolina, wrote, "I am grateful for a bark park to take my dog-children to, so I picked up extra poop and trash this morning." Mary, from Philadelphia wrote, "I am so grateful for the beautiful snow outside."

Gratitude floats our boats and moves us to do all kinds of things inspired by joy. Gratitude can help us transform our fears into courage, our anger into forgiveness, our isolation into belonging, and another's pain into healing. Saying "Thank you every day will create feelings of love, compassion, and hope.

But the fact is, the art of living—for that is what we speak about when we speak of gratitude—isn't something that comes naturally to most people. Most of us need to work intentionally to increase the intensity, duration, and frequency of positive, grateful feelings—a daunting challenge indeed. But fear not, this workbook

is here to help! Inside we have provided you with
mindful meditations, hands-on exercises, profound
practices, inspiring quotations, space for writing,
thought-provoking questions, and even positive "power
tools" that will help you build a more grateful life. Becca
Anderson's book is one I will turn to on a daily basis.
To master the art of being a gratitude practitioner, you
have to take time for gratitude every day; that works for
me and it will work for you. You'll be glad and oh-so-
thankful you did.

Introduction

Dear Reader,

Gratitude is one of the loveliest paths to personal growth. It can be subtle; after contemplating what it is to approach your life-thankfulness, you may find that you have the "half-full mindset." Maybe instead of worrying Sunday nights about work and meetings and goals, you relax and remember to be grateful to have work you really enjoy. Next thing you know, your co-workers picked up on the fact that you were less stressed out and more fun to be around, and your desk becomes on oasis of positivity in the office and people leave your workspace with a spring in their step. Your family responded in kind, and your home is a calmer, happier place filled with calmer, happier people. Your friends who used to call you and complain about life now call and tell you all the good things happening. That one took a while but your aura of gratefulness eventually took hold and bloomed.

13

You, my friend, have an attitude of gratitude and are
making the world a better place.
Well done, and please allow me to be the first to say
thank you. I guarantee you, I won't be the last. I am a
big one for setting intentions and do so every morning.
I intend you grow and soar in your wisdom and, if
some of the ideas, quotes, and suggestions from the
"gratitude gurus" included in this book inspire you, all
the better.

Blessings to you on your journey,

Becca

Power Thoughts:
A Thankful Way
of Life

Gratitude and esteem are good
foundations of affection.
—Jane Austen

'Enough' is a feast.
—Buddhist Proverb

When you arise in the morning,
think of what a precious privilege
it is to be alive—to breathe, to
think, to enjoy, to love.
—Marcus Aurelius

I have found that worry and
irritation vanish the moment
when I open my mind to the
many blessing that I possess.
—Dale Carnegie

It is impossible to feel grateful
and depressed in the same
moment.
—Naomi Williams

15

Chapter One

January – Time for Renewal

How to Have an Attitude of Gratitude

1.

Be grateful and recognize the things
others have done to help you.

2.

When you say "thank you" to someone,
it signals what you appreciate
and why you appreciate it.

3.

Post a "Thank you to all" on your Facebook page or your
blog, or send individual e-mails to friends, family,
and colleagues.

4.

Send a handwritten thank you note.
These are noteworthy because so few of us
take time to write and mail them.

5.

Think thoughts of gratitude—two or three good things that
happened today—and notice calm settle through your
head, at least for a moment.
It activates a part of the brain that floods the body with
endorphins, or feel-good hormones.

6.

Remember the ways your life has been made easier
or better because of others' efforts. Be aware of and
acknowledge the good things, large and small,
going on around you.

7.

Keep a gratitude journal or set aside time each day or evening to list the people or things you're grateful for today. The list may start out short, but it will grow as you notice more of the good things around you.

8.

Being grateful shakes you out of self-absorption and helps you recognize those who've done wonderful things for you. Expressing that gratitude continues to draw those people into your sphere.

9.

Remember this thought from Maya Angelou: "When you learn, teach; when you get, give."

10.

Join forces to do good. If you have survived illness or loss, you may want to reach out to others to help as a way of showing gratitude for those who reached out to you.

11.

As the old Jimmy Durante song goes, "make someone happy." A thoughtful, handwritten letter will do that EVERY TIME!

It's so important to make
someone happy.

Make just one someone happy...
Fame, if you win it,
Comes and goes in a minutes.
Where's the real stuff in life, to
cling to?
Love is the answer!

Make someone happy,
Make just one someone happy.
And you will be happy too.

12.

No kind action ever stops with itself. One kind action
leads to another. Good example is followed. A single act
of kindness throws out roots in all directions, and the
roots spring up and make new trees.
The greatest work that kindness does to others
is that it makes them kind themselves.

—Amelia Earhart

13.

Every great dream begins with a dreamer. Always
remember, you have within you the strength, the patience,
and the passion to reach for the stars to change the world.

—Harriet Tubman

14.

Let us be grateful to the people who make us happy;
they are the charming gardeners
who make our souls blossom.

—Marcel Proust

15.

Even though he had a Very Small Heart, it could hold
a rather large amount of Gratitude.

—A.A. Milne

16.

True happiness is to enjoy the present, without anxious
dependence upon the future, not to amuse ourselves
with either hopes or fears but to rest satisfied with
what we have.

—Seneca

17.

Gratitude is not only the greatest of virtues,
but the parent of all others.

—Cicero

18.

Appreciation is a wonderful thing. It makes what is
excellent in others belong to us as well.

—Voltaire

19.

Gratitude looks to the Past and love to the Present.

—C.S. Lewis

20.

In normal life we hardly realize how much more we receive than we give, and life cannot be rich without such gratitude.

—Dietrich Bonhoeffer

21.

We can only be said to be alive in those moments when our hearts are conscious of our treasures.

—Thornton Wilder

22.

The unthankful heart discovers no mercies; but the thankful heart will find, in every hour, some heavenly blessings.

—Henry Ward Beecher

23.

Gratitude is a divine emotion. It fills the heart, not to
bursting; it warms it, but not to fever. I like to taste
leisurely of bliss. Devoured in haste,
I do not know its flavor.

—Charlotte Bronte

24.

Take full account of what Excellencies you possess,
and in gratitude remember how you would hanker after
them, if you had them not.

—Marcus Aurelius

25.

Courtesies of a small and trivial character are the ones
which strike deepest in the grateful
and appreciating heart.

—Henry Clay

Choose to Be Happy

This is your life; only you can truly control your choices, and choosing thankfulness and happiness is the best way to achieve being a good to yourself as well as the world. Here are some suggestions for how you can ensure simple joy in your life:

- •Be the best you can be by your own standards
- •Surround yourself with people who inspire you and make you feel good
- •Focus on what you have, not what you lack
- •Optimism trumps pessimism every time!
- •Smile often and genuinely
- •Be honest, to yourself and to others
- •Help others
- •Embrace your past, live in the present, and look forward for what is yet to come

28

26.

Be happy, noble heart, be blessed for all the good thou hast done and wilt do hereafter, and let my gratitude remain in obscurity like your good deeds.

—Alexandre Dumas

27.

If you count all your assets, you always show a profit.

—Robert Quillen

28.

The soul that gives thanks can find comfort in everything; the soul that complains can find comfort in nothing.

—Hannah Whitall Smith

29.

The essence of all beautiful art, all great art,
is gratitude.

—Friedrich Nietzsche

30.

Gratitude is happiness doubled by wonder.

—GK Chesterton

31.

The worship most acceptable to God comes from
a thankful and cheerful heart.

—Plutarch

Teaching Gratitude

Teach your children well. Sit down with your child and ask him or her to create a talk about thankfulness. Provide a simple starting point: "Thank you for..." Then ask your child to draw a picture to go with the concept and get started writing the first of MANY thank you notes for years to come!

32.

I awoke this morning with devout thanksgiving for my
friends, the old and the new.

—Ralph Waldo Emerson

33.

Sometimes I go about pitying myself, and all the while I am
being carried across the sky by beautiful clouds.

—Ojibway proverb

34.

When I'm not thank'd at all, I'm thank'd enough,
I've done my duty, and I've done no more.

—Henry Fielding

35.

Do not let the empty cup be your first teacher of the blessings you had when it was full.

—Alexander Maclaren

36.

A grateful mind
By owing owes not, but still pays, at once
Indebted and discharg'd.

—John Milton

37.

Thankfulness is the tune of angels.

—Edmund Spenser

38.

Praise the bridge that carried you over.

—George Colman the Younger

39.

Let the man, who would be grateful, think of repaying
a kindness, even while receiving it.

—Seneca the Younger

40.

Ingratitude calls forth reproaches as gratitude brings
renewed kindnesses.

—Marie de Rabutin-Chantal, marquise de Sévigné

41.

From too much love of living,
From hope and fear set free,
We thank with brief thanksgiving
Whatever gods may be.

—Algernon Charles Swinburne

Unplug
(and Recharge!)

Forego using technological devices today. Texting your friend, watching your favorite show, checking your email—all can wait until tomorrow! Turn off your devices and turn on your senses! Read a book, cook a meal, and enjoy the outdoors by taking a walk or tending to your garden. Technology distracts us from the real world, occupying our attention with game applications, chat rooms, social media websites, commercials, and so on. Want to know what's going on in the news? Read a newspaper. Be aware of the here and now by finding activities that don't require electricity or a battery. Make your own entertainment!

36

Chapter Two

February – Matters of the Heart

Practice Random Acts of Kindness and Senseless Acts of Beauty

Random Acts of Kindness Day is always the week of Valentine's Day. I always love to hear how this meaningful movement has touched others' lives. Have you seen those bumper stickers, the ones encouraging you to commit "random acts of kindness?" What they can't tell you in that little space is how performing those acts can be a way of transforming yourself. When you begin to focus on extending kindness toward others, you'll feel more kindness coming toward you. Not only will you make someone else's day better, you'll be surprised at how well yours improves. It's rather like the "Secret Santa" gift exchange that many offices and families adopt during the weeks leading up to Christmas. There is delight when you do something for another while keeping your identity a secret. When you watch a person receiving a surprise gift, you see her face change, eyes open wide with delight, a smile bursting into a grin, and laughter erupting. The person appears to feel sheer joy at the unexpected. The old adage is true: "It is in giving that we receive."

1.

For love casts out fear, and gratitude can conquer pride.

—Louisa May Alcott

2.

Let us rise up and be thankful,
for if we didn't learn a lot today,
at least we learned a little.

—Buddha

3.

Thankfulness is the beginning of gratitude. Gratitude
is the completion of thankfulness. Thankfulness may
consist merely of words. Gratitude is shown in acts.

—Henri Frederic Amiel

4.

You cannot do a kindness too soon because you never know how soon it will be too late.

—Ralph Waldo Emerson

5.

Do not spoil what you have by desiring what you have not; remember that what you now have was once among the things you only hoped for.

—Epicurus

6.

One looks back with appreciation to the brilliant teachers, but with gratitude to those who touched our human feelings.

—Carl Jung

7.

Joy is the simplest form of gratitude.

—Karl Barth

8.

No one is useless in this world who lightens
the burden of another.

—Charles Dickens

9.

If the only prayer you say in your life is "Thank You,"
that would suffice.

—Meister Eckhart

10.

Silent gratitude isn't much good to anyone.

—Gertrude Stein

11.

Charity never humiliated him who profited from it,
nor ever bound him by the chains of gratitude, since it was
not to him but to God that the gift was made.

—Antoine de Saint-Exupéry

12.

Gratitude is the inward feeling of kindness received.
Thankfulness is the natural impulse to express that
feeling. Thanksgiving is the following of that impulse.

—Henry Van Dyke

13.

Some people grumble that roses have thorns;
I am grateful that thorns have roses.

—Jean Baptiste Alphonse Karr

14.

They do not love that do not show their love.

—William Shakespeare

Let Your Love Shine

Following are some ideas for you to consider during this month that celebrate love. As you know, this isn't all about romance, but everyone who touches your heart and is deserving of a shout out: relatives, coworkers, neighbors, good friends, your children, and even strangers offering random acts of kindness. As they say, love is what makes the world go 'round.

I Just Called To Say I Love You

Call your parents (or whoever raised you) and thank them for everything they did for you!

Service men and women are doing just that, SERVICE. And they should be thanked for it. Many of these noble souls are very far away and receive little mail to their camp or barrack. Take a few moments to acknowledge their contribution and offer a friendly hello from back home in the USA. You can learn all about Operation Write Home at www.operationwritehome.gov. I have heard of great pen pal relationships come out of this gesture of gratitude, too.

Love Notes

Leave encouraging, inspiring, or funny notes/quotes in a library book or other random places (without littering or defiling public property). A simple note stapled to a bulletin board, taped to a column, or written in chalk on the sidewalk may influence in wonderful ways—plus, you'll be like a secret agent, bringing happiness to others. This website has fun examples that might give you an idea: www.artofgettingstarted.com

Valentine's Day

It's that sometimes-anticipated-by-couples-yet-often-dreaded-by-singles day of the year! In the spirit of Valentine's Day, send an anonymous letter or bouquet of flowers to someone special to you—your mom, your recently divorced best friend. This deliberate act of kindness will last long after the 14th as the memory lingers on.

Offer to watch a friend or neighbor's children so they can run errands or spend time with their significant other. A really nice thing to do the night before Valentine's Day, by the way.

15.

The world is more malleable than you think and it's waiting for you to hammer it into shape.

—Bono

16.

He is a wise man who does not grieve for the things which he has not, but rejoices for those which he has.

—Epictetus

17.

Gratitude is the sign of noble souls.

—Aesop

18.

Train yourself never to put off the word or action for
the expression of gratitude.

—Albert Schweitzer

19.

Gratitude changes the pangs of memory into
a tranquil joy.

—Dietrich Bonhoeffer

20.

If you have lived, take thankfully the past.

—John Dryden

21.

Gratitude is the moral memory of mankind.

—Georg Simmel

22.

To be happy at home is the ultimate result
of all ambition.

—Samuel Johnson

23.

When it comes to life the critical thing is whether you
take things for granted or take them with gratitude.

—G. K. Chesterton

How Thank You Notes Can Change the World

Write a note of gratitude, a "mindful memo," to the people in your everyday life who make a difference—the mailman, a grocery clerk, or the greeter at the mall. Tell your friends about their places of business or their great service so their businesses can grow. Just by paying attention to those people in your everyday life, who can so easily go unnoticed (especially if your smartphone is glued to your hand), you can enrich each other's lives a little each day.

24.

When eating bamboo sprouts, remember the man
who planted them.

—Chinese Proverb

25.

The mere habit of learning to love is the thing.

—**Jane Austen**

26.

For one man who thanks God that he is not
as other men there are a thousand to offer thanks that
they are as other men, sufficiently as others
are to escape attention.

—**John Dewey**

27.

Gratitude is one of the least articulate of the emotions, especially when it is deep.

—Felix Frankfurter

28.

Leap Day! Make sure to spend that extra day doing something you love and make it productive. What did you need to get done yesterday that didn't?
Here is one great way to spend that day: cruise over to www.myphilanthropedia.org to find your perfect match of an organization to donate to or volunteer with.
I learned about this from a TED Talk and discovered this vital service: Philanthropedia rate verified, financially responsible charities according to how much great work they're doing. Donate to top nonprofits in a cause you care about.

Don't Be Judgmental; Be Kind Just Because You Can

It's easy to judge others for their actions and take for granted those we love or meet in chance encounters. We sometimes get so caught up in our busy-ness that we forget others are busy, too; they have rough days just like us, and they benefit from our kindnesses just as we do theirs. Go out of your way to smile at strangers, say good morning, say thank you, give a compliment, and listen attentively to someone who needs your ear. Do it because you can, because it feels great, because it makes someone else feel good. Don't worry about a subsequent thank you; let a thank you be a beautiful perk, rather than an expectation.

Chapter Three

March - The Season of Change

What Can You Change About Your Life in One Day?

Take stock of your day-to-day life. Are you giving to others or is it a little out of balance, where your work or your immediately family gets 99% of what you offer the world? You can change that in one day. Donate more of your time or money to a charity. Supporting a cause will help keep you informed about social issues and can strengthen your sense of well-being while benefitting others in the process. Additionally, monetary donations are tax-deductible. This is really just a bonus, because the real reward is not on April 15th but comes the other 364 days of the year.

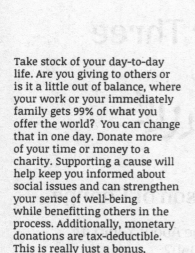

1.

Gratitude is the fairest blossom which
springs from the soul.

—Henry Ward Beecher

2.

Gratitude is the memory of the heart.

—French Proverb

3.

I murmured because I had no shoes,
until I met a man who had no feet.

—Persian Proverb

4.

The knowledge that something remains yet unenjoyed
impairs our enjoyment of the good before us.

—Samuel Johnson

5.

If a fellow isn't thankful for what he's got, he isn't likely to
be thankful for what he's going to get.

—Frank A. Clark

6.

The roots of all goodness lie in the soil of appreciation
for goodness.

—The Dalai Lama

7.

Appreciation can change a day, even change a life. Your willingness to put it into words is all that is necessary.

—Margaret Cousins

8.

There are only two ways to live your life. One is as though nothing is a miracle. The other is as though everything is a miracle.

—Albert Einstein

9.

Give thanks for a little and you will find a lot.

—The Hausa of Nigeria

A Day Without Laughter is a Day Wasted

As the wise sage Charlie Chaplin said, "A day without laughter is a day wasted." Laughter and good humor are infectious. Sharing a funny story or memory with others helps to bind people together, increasing happiness and intimacy between friends, acquaintances, and loved ones. According to www.helpguide.org, laughter triggers happiness and can strengthen the immune system, boost energy, relieve physical and emotional pain, and battle the effects of stress. The more you laugh, the less you need to see the doctor. Today is a great day—let yourself enjoy it.

10.

Now is no time to think of what you do not have. Think of what you can do with what there is.

—Ernest Hemingway

11.

A grateful mind is a great mind which eventually attracts to itself great things.

—Plato

12.

Thou who hast given so much to me, give me one more thing... a grateful heart!

—George Herbert

13.

They are not poor that have little, but they that desire much. The richest man, whatever his lot, is the one who's content with his lot.

—Dutch Proverb

14.

If you can't reward then you should thank.

—Arabic Proverb

15.

You have no cause for anything but gratitude and joy.

—Buddha

Practice Random Acts of Kindness (and deliberate ones, too)

The Hebrew word mitzvah means a good deed or an act of kindness. Judaism teaches that the world is built on kindness. I recall what my Bobbie, a dear friend in Salt Lake City who was my son's first caregiver, used to tell me about the importance of doing mitzvahs. She believes in the power of doing something good for another person but not telling them about it. She is a perfect example of someone who practices random acts of kindness, and also one who sees and acknowledges the beauty in everyone she meets. I always feel better just by being in her presence. Entire campaigns focused on practicing random acts of kindness have sprouted up. This, along with "having an attitude of gratitude," enriches my days in many ways. There are myriad ways you can practice

63

random acts of kindness. Don't forget to include yourself when you are doing them!

- Pick up trash you see on the street and make the world a better place.
- Pay for the coffee of the person behind you in line.
- Buy a cookie for a coworker and leave it on their desk.
- Hold the door open for someone.
- Smile at a stranger.
- Send a thank you note through the mail.

16.

Religion is grace and ethics is gratitude.

—Thomas Erskine

17.

Gratitude bestows reverence, allowing us to encounter everyday epiphanies, those transcendent moments of awe that change forever how we experience life and the world.

—John Milton

18.

Gratitude is a currency that we can mint for ourselves, and spend without fear of bankruptcy.

—Fred De Witt Van Amburgh

19.

Gratitude is like the good faith of traders: it maintains commerce, and we often pay, not because it is just to discharge our debts, but that we may more readily find people to trust us.

—Francois de la Rochefoucald

20.

You may believe anything that is good of a grateful man.

—Thomas Fuller

21.

Sweet music's melting fall, but sweeter yet / the still small voice of gratitude.

—Thomas Gray

22.

No metaphysician ever felt the deficiency of language
so much as the grateful.

—**C.C. Colton**

23.

When our perils are past, shall our gratitude sleep?
No – here's to the pilot that weathered the storm.

—**George Canning**

To Be Of Use

"To Be of Use," Marge Piercy's marvelous poem, suggests something of the human condition—that we all long to be useful, to help, to work together toward a common goal. This is surely the best part of the human spirit. Meditate upon this:

What is my true purpose? What am I here to do in this life?

I recommend that you contemplate this question deeply and for a very long time—days, weeks, months, and years even. Let the answer speak through your service to others.

24.

I am grateful for what I am and have.
My thanksgiving is perpetual.

—Henry David Thoreau

25.

We have been the recipients of the choicest
bounties of Heaven.

—Abraham Lincoln

26.

The thankful receiver bears a plentiful harvest.

—William Blake

27.

When you arise in the morning, give thanks for the morning light, for your life and strength. Give thanks for your food, and the joy of living. If you see no reason for giving thanks, the fault lies with yourself.

—Tecumseh, Shawnee Chief

28.

If you cannot be grateful for what you have received, then be thankful for what you have been spared.

—Yiddish Proverb

29.

Be content with what you have; rejoice in the way things are. When you realize there is nothing lacking, the world belongs to you.

—Lao-Tzu

30.

Whatever I am offered in devotion with a pure heart —
a leaf, a flower, fruit, or water — I accept with joy.

—Bhagavad Gita

31.

He that is hard to please may get nothing in the end.

—Aesop

Be Kind to Yourself, Too

Make a commitment to yourself to refrain from negative self-talk. Be kind to yourself and focus on the traits you like rather than the ones you don't. The extremely wise Dawna Markova, the author of some of my favorite books, including I Will Not Die an Unlived Life, says, "Your soul remembers when you put yourself down; it imprints upon you. Never do this. Self-compassion is key to a life well-lived."

Chapter Four

April - Hope Springs Eternal

Be of Good Will

The Little Things Count: Do little things for others, like holding the door open and letting them go before you, or allowing the person with only one item go ahead of you at the grocery store. I think this is due to our over-busy-ness, but nowadays, so many people rush through life and don't consider the feelings of others. A simple gesture can be a good reminder for us all, myself included. Take your time, look around you; how can you help someone today? In the end, you are also helping yourself just as much.

1.

Forget injuries, never forget kindness.

—Confucius

2.

Gratitude is heaven itself.

—William Blake

3.

**Ingratitude is the most abominable of sins...For it is a
forgetting of the graces, benefits,
and blessings received.**

—St Ignatius Loyola

4.

Gratitude therefore takes nothing for granted, is never unresponsive, is constantly awakening to new wonder, and to praise of the goodness of God. For the grateful person knows that God is good, not by hearsay but by experience. And that is what makes all the difference.

—Thomas Merton

5.

The poor man shuddered, overflowed with an angelic joy; he declared in his transport that this would last through life; he said to himself that he really had not suffered enough to deserve such radiant happiness, and he thanked God, in the depths of his soul, for having permitted that he, a miserable man, should be so loved.

—Victor Hugo

6.

The smallest act of kindness is worth more than the grandest intention.

—Oscar Wilde

7.

A tree is known by its fruit; a man by his deeds. A good deed is never lost; he who sows courtesy reaps friendship, and he who plants kindness gathers love.

—St. Saint Basil

8.

Gratitude is a vaccine, an antitoxin and an antiseptic.

—John Henry Jowett

9.

I arise this day / with love in my heart / through the warmth of the sun, / the radiance of the moon, / freedom of the wind, / joy of rushing water, / splendor of fire, / stability of earth, / serenity of stars, and / the wisdom of silence. / I embrace this day / through the grace of life to guide me / and the promise of love to inspire me.

—Irish Prayer

10.

I didn't expect to recover from my second operation but since I did, I consider that I'm living on borrowed time. Every day that dawns is a gift to me and I take it in that way. I accept it gratefully without looking beyond it. I completely forget my physical suffering and all the unpleasantness of my present condition and I think only of the joy of seeing the sun rise once more and of being able to work a little bit, even under difficult conditions.

—Henri Matisse

11.

It is only normal that / People count losses with / their minds, / and ignore / to count blessings / with the graciousness / of their hearts.

—Suzy Kassem

12.

Give thanks
For what had been given to you,
However little.
Be pure, never falter.

—Buddha

13.

Gratitude is not only the greatest of virtues,
but the parents of all the others.

—Marcus Tullius Cicero

14.

Feeling gratitude and not expressing it is like wrapping a
present and not giving it.

—William Arthur Ward

15.

Gratitude unlocks the fullness of life. It turns what
we have into enough, and more. It turns denial into
acceptance, chaos to order, confusion to clarity. It
can turn a meal into a feast, a house into a home, a
stranger into a friend. Gratitude makes sense of our
past, brings peace for today and creates
a vision for tomorrow.

—Melody Beattie

No Strings Attached

Write down the things that someone has given you, no strings attached, for which you are grateful. It can be an old sofa, some sound advice, or a lift to the airport. Now list ten things you would like to give someone yourself, and see how many of those things you can cross off in a week.

Examples:

- Drive a friend to the airport
- Carry groceries for an elder to their car
- Babysit for a relative
- Buy a friend a cup of coffee
- Volunteer at a soup kitchen

16.

Thankfulness is the beginning of gratitude. Gratitude is the completion of thankfulness. Thankfulness may consist merely of words. Gratitude is shown in acts.

—Henri Frederic Amiel

17.

Gratitude helps you to grow and expand; gratitude brings JOY and laughter into your life and into the lives of all those around you.

—Eileen Caddy

18.

Gratitude can transform common days into thanksgivings, turn routine jobs into joy and change ordinary opportunities into blessings.

—William Arthur Ward

19.

As we express our gratitude, we must never forget that the highest appreciation is not to utter words, but to live by them.

—John F. Kennedy

20.

Let us be grateful to people who make us happy; they are the charming gardeners who make our souls blossom.

—Marcel Proust

21.

Cultivate the habit of being grateful for every good thing that comes to you, and to give thanks continuously.

—Ralph Waldo Emerson

Get Out of Your Head and Back Into Your Heart

Because the world we live in today is very much about getting in your head and staying there, many of us have to make a concentrated effort to become grounded and in touch with our bodies and the natural world around us. Grounding is the technique for centering you within your being, getting into your body and out of your head. Grounding is the way we reconnect and balance ourselves through the power of the element of earth. When you see someone driving past talking on their cell phone, you know they are not grounded. For deep grounding, we recommend a creative visualization or, better yet, a group guided meditation.

This is the simplest of rituals; one you can do every day of your life. As you walk, take the time to look and really see what is in your path. For example, my friend Eileen takes a bag with her and picks up every piece of garbage in her path. She does this as an act of love for the earth. During the ten years she has practiced this ritual, she has probably turned a mountain of garbage into recycled glass, paper, and plastic. Eileen is VERY grounded. She is also a happy person who exudes and shares joy to all in her path.

22.

Thankfulness is the beginning of gratitude. Gratitude
is the completion of thankfulness. Thankfulness may
consist merely of words. Gratitude is shown in acts.

—Henri Frederic Amiel

23.

Reflect upon your present blessings—of which every man
has many—not on your past misfortunes,
of which all men have some.

—Charles Dickens

24.

You simply will not be the same person two months
from now after consciously giving thanks each day
for the abundance that exists in your life. And you will
have set in motion an ancient spiritual law: the more
you have and are grateful for,
the more will be given you.

—Sara Ban Breathnach

25.

Happiness cannot be traveled to, owned, earned, worn or consumed. Happiness is the spiritual experience of living every minute with love, grace and gratitude.

—Denis Waitley

26.

Make it a habit to tell people thank you. To express your appreciation, sincerely and without the expectation of anything in return. Truly appreciate those around you, and you'll soon find many others around you. Truly appreciate life, and you'll find that you have more of it.

—Ralph Marston

27.

No one who achieves success does so without acknowledging the help of others. The wise and confident acknowledge this help with gratitude.

—Alfred North Whitehead

28.

You say grace before meals. All right. But I say grace
before the concert and the opera, and grace before the
play and pantomime, and grace before I open a book,
and grace before sketching, painting, swimming,
fencing, boxing, walking, playing, dancing and grace
before I dip the pen in the ink.

—G.K. Chesterton

29.

How wonderful it would be if we could help our children
and grandchildren to learn thanksgiving at an early
age. Thanksgiving opens the doors. It changes a child's
personality. A child is resentful, negative—or thankful.
Thankful children want to give,
they radiate happiness, they draw people.

—Sir John Templeton

30.

The best way to show my gratitude is to accept
everything, even my problems, with joy.

—Mother Teresa

Chapter Five

May - The Merriest Month

Simple Acts of Gratitude and Goodness

Live Aloha

In the beautiful paradise known as the Hawaiian Islands, there is a tradition of "Living Aloha." This one encompasses all of the aforementioned good deeds, which is why it's the most important of all. In the Hawaiian tradition, "aloha" stands for the akahai, lokahi, olu`olu, ha`aha`a, and ahonui—in English, these words translate to kindness, bringing unity, politeness, humbled, and enduring. If you live your life with simple acts of goodness every day and follow the tradition of native Hawaiian islanders, you will surely become a good in the world.

1.

Appreciation can make a day—even change a life. Your willingness to it into words is all that is necessary.

—Margaret Cousins

2.

Gratitude is the pillow upon which you kneel to say your nightly prayer, and let faith be the bridge you build to overcome evil and welcome good.

—Maya Angelou

3.

The more one does and sees and feels, the more one is able to do, and the more genuine may be ones appreciation of fundamental things like home, and love and understanding companionship.

—Amelia Earhart

4.

Let us rise up and be thankful, for if we didn't learn a lot today, at least we learned a little, and if we didn't learn a little, at least we didn't get sick, and if we got sick, at least we didn't die; so, let us all be thankful.

—Buddha

5.

He is a wise man who does not grieve for the things, which he has not, but rejoices for those which he has.

—Epictetus

6.

Gratitude is the fairest blossom which springs from the soul.

—Henry Ward Beecher

7.

When we become more fully aware that our success is due in large measure to the loyalty, helpfulness, and encouragement we have received from others, our desire grows to pass on similar gifts. Gratitude spurs us on to prove ourselves worthy of what others have done for us. The spirit of gratitude is a powerful energizer.

—Wilferd A. Peterson

8.

We make a living by what we get; we make a life by what we give.

—Winston Churchill

9.

Wear gratitude like a cloak and it will feed every corner of your life.

—Rumi

10.

Gratitude is when memory is stored in the heart
and not in the mind.

—Lionel Hampton

11.

As we express our gratitude, we must never forget that the
highest appreciation is not to utter words but
to live by them.

—John F Kennedy

12.

Gratitude is riches. Complaint is poverty.

—Doris Day

13.

As each day comes to us refreshed and anew, so does
my gratitude renews itself daily. The breaking of the
sun over the horizon is my grateful heart dawning
upon a blessed world.

—Terri Guillemets

14.

Gratitude is merely the secret hope of further favors.

—François de La Rochefoucauld

15.

With arms outstretched I thank.
With heart beating gratefully I love.
With body in health I jump for joy.
With spirit full I live.

—Terri Guillemets

List Your Life

Instead of writing up and crossing things off of a "bucket list," create a "life list." Let your hopes, dreams, fears, and thoughts spill out of you and into this list. Next to each entry, write down how that emotion or fear makes you feel—does it hold you back or empower you? This task will put you on the road to self-discovery. Knowing who you are is important in order to have relationships with others. Know thyself:

1. Your hopes
2. Your dreams
3. What you love
4. What you are grateful for

16.

The unthankful heart discovers no mercies; but the
thankful heart will find, in every hour,
some heavenly blessings.

—Anonymous

17.

Not what we say about our blessings, but how we use
them, is the true measure of our thanksgiving.

—W.T. Purkiser

18.

In ordinary life we hardly realize that we receive a
great deal more than we give, and that it is only with
gratitude that life becomes rich.

——Dietrich Bonhoeffer

19.

If you look to others for fulfillment, you will never be fulfilled. If your happiness depends on money, you will never be happy with yourself. Be content with what you have; rejoice in the way things are. When you realize there is nothing lacking, the world belongs to you.

—Lao Tzu

20.

Do not indulge in dreams of having what you have not, but reckon up the chief of the blessings you do possess, and then thankfully remember how you would crave for them if they were not yours.

—Marcus Aurelius

21.

Nothing more detestable does the earth produce than an ungrateful man.

—Decimus Magnus Ausonius

Go Ahead and Make Someone's Day

The groundbreaking psychologist William James, brother of the great novelist Henry James, stated, "The deepest principle in human nature is the craving to be appreciated." If you think about it, you know how wonderful it feels to be acknowledged. Let someone know that you appreciate having him or her in your life. Sometimes we forget how good it feels to be appreciated; yet we know how lousy it feels to be unappreciated. Go ahead and tell someone how thankful you are for his or her presence in your life; it will only make you closer.

22.

He who is not contented with what he has, would not
be contented with what he would like to have.

—Socrates

23.

God gave you a gift of 86,400 seconds today. Have you
used one to say 'thank you?'

—William A. Ward

24.

Gratitude is an art of painting an adversity into
a lovely picture.

—Kak Sri

25.

As each day comes to us refreshed and anew, so does
my gratitude renew itself daily. The breaking of the sun
over the horizon is my grateful heart dawning
upon a blessed world.

—Terri Guillemets

26.

If you want to turn your life around, try thankfulness. It
will change your life mightily.

—Gerald Good

27.

I can no other answer make, but thanks,
thanks, thanks.

—William Shakespeare

28.

Gratitude is the least of the virtues, but ingratitude
is the worst of vices.

—Thomas Fuller

29.

Who does not thank for little will not thank for much.

—Estonian Proverb

30.

Thou hast given so much to me, Give one thing more,
- a grateful heart; Not thankful when it pleaseth me,
As if Thy blessings had spare days, But such a heart
whose pulse may be Thy praise.

—George Herbert

Rewire Your Brain To Be More Positive

Neuropsychiatrist David Amen, MD, posits that thoughts carry physical properties and that the properties of negative thoughts can be detrimental to you leading a healthy, happy life. To overturn these negative effects, he prescribes thinking more positively, maintaining that by doing so, you can change the way your brain works and in turn change your life for the better.

Chapter Six

June - Life is in Full Bloom

The Art of Appreciation

Don't Just Go Through It, Grow Through It

An attitude of gratitude can make a profound difference in our day-to-day lives, yet, as we all come to know, not every day is filled with all good things. We each endure difficult passages: illnesses, money trouble, work woes, relationship issues, the loss of a loved one, and countless others. These are the vicissitudes of life. However, it is the attitude you bring to each situation that makes all the difference. Share what you learned from others from your life lessons and offer it if you think it can be of help to a fellow traveler who is walking a hard path.

1.

Gratitude is the most exquisite form of courtesy.

—Jacques Maritain

2.

When you are grateful, fear disappears and
abundance appears.

—Tony Robbins

3.

Gratitude brings warmth to the giver
and the receiver alike.

—Elder Robert D. Hales

4.

Showing gratitude is one of the simplest yet most powerful things humans can do for each other.

—Randy Pausch

5.

Gratitude is the ability to experience life as a gift. It liberates us from the prison of self-preoccupation.

—John Ortberg

6.

People travel to wonder at the height of mountains, at the huge waves of the sea at the long courses of rivers, at the vast compass of the ocean, at the circular motion of the stars; and they pass by themselves without wondering... Now, let us acknowledge the wonder of our physical incarnation—that we are here, in these particular bodies, at this particular time, in these particular circumstances. May we never take for granted the gift of our individuality.

—Saint Augustine

7.

Gratitude is the sign of noble souls.

—Aesop

8.

Thankfulness is the beginning of gratitude. Gratitude is the completion of thankfulness. Thankfulness may consist merely of words. Gratitude is shown in acts.

—Henri Frédéric Amiel

9.

To speak gratitude is courteous and pleasant, to enact gratitude is generous and noble, but to live gratitude is to touch Heaven.

—Johannes A. Gaertner

10.

We tend to forget that happiness doesn't come as a result of getting something we don't have, but rather of recognizing and appreciating what we do have.

—Fredrick Koeing

11.

Find the light. Reach for it. Live for it. Pull yourself up by it. Gratitude always makes for straighter, taller trees.

—Al R. Young

12.

Gratitude is the sweetest thing in a seeker's life—in all human life. If there is gratitude in your heart, then there will be tremendous sweetness in your eyes.

—Sri Chinmoy

13.

You cannot exercise much power without gratitude
because it is gratitude that keeps you
connected with power.

—Wallace Wattles

14.

To educate yourself for the feeling of gratitude means to
take nothing for granted, but to always seek out and value
the kind that will stand behind the action. Nothing that is
done for you is a matter of course. Everything originates
in a will for the good, which is directed at you.
Train yourself never to put off the word or action
for the expression of gratitude.

—Albert Schweitzer

15.

Gratitude is pure happiness. Happiness is
pure perfection.

——Hugh Prather

Love the Ones You're With

I have seen this excellent exercise put into practice at work, family reunions, and dinner parties. It never fails to bring a group of people closer, and it brings out the best in anyone. It is especially effective among a group of fractious folk, and it calms roiling waters easily. Time your moment well; never at the beginning of a get-together. Whenever there is a lull would be best. Call everyone to attention and say you want to acknowledge your appreciation for the group.

Do so with simple statements. Examples: "What I appreciate about Rich is his humility; he is brilliant but never showy."

"What I appreciate about Nancy is her kindness and generosity. She helped me out when I was in a bad way. I will always be grateful to her for that."

Offer a positive appreciation for each person and encourage others to do the same. Talk about a "turnaround"—this can turn stormy skies blue in five minutes flat.

16.

True gratitude can never come from the mind. It has to
flow from the heart to the mind and the body.
Until everything we have and everything we are
is a sea of gratitude.

—Sri Chinmoy

17.

If you have true gratitude, it will express itself
automatically. It will be visible in your eyes, around your
being, in your aura. It is like the fragrance of a flower. In
most cases if there is a beautiful flower, the fragrance will
be there naturally. The flower and its fragrance cannot be
separated.

—Sri Chinmoy

18.

Two kinds of gratitude: The sudden kind we feel for
what we take; the larger kind we feel for what we give.

—Edwin Arlington Robinson

19.

When I started counting my blessings,
my whole life turned around.

—Willie Nelson

20.

Give thanks for a little and you will find a lot.

—Nigerian Proverb

21.

The further I wake into this life, the more I realize that
God is everywhere and the extraordinary is waiting
quietly beneath the skin of all that is ordinary. Light is
in both the broken bottle and the diamond, and music
is in both the flowing violin and the water dripping
from the drainage pipe. Yes, God is under the porch
as well as on top of the mountain, and joy is in both
the front row and the bleachers, if we are willing to be
where we are.

—Mark Nepo

Be a Candle

Sometimes we all feel deflated
or overwhelmed, someone
or something hurts us or
disappoints us, or we hear bad
news about a loved one's medical
condition. On those days, when
you feel your light has gone out,
remember there is always a
glimmer of hope and something
to be thankful for. You can be
a light for others in dark days.
Albert Schweitzer said it well:
"Sometimes our light goes out,
but is blown again into instant
flame by an encounter with
another human being. Each of
us owes the deepest thanks to
those who have rekindled this
inner light."

22.

It is necessary, then, to cultivate the habit of being grateful for every good thing that comes to you, and to give thanks continuously. And because all things have contributed to your advancement, you should include all things in your gratitude.

—Wallace D. Wattles

23.

It is not joy that makes us grateful; it is gratitude that makes us joyful.

—David Steindl-Rast

24.

Silent gratitude isn't much use to anyone.

—G.B. Stern

25.

Happiness is itself a kind of gratitude.

—Joseph Wood Krutch

26.

There is calmness to a life lived in gratitude, a quiet joy.

—Ralph H. Blum

27.

If you concentrate on finding whatever is good in every situation, you will discover that your life will suddenly be filled with gratitude, a feeling that nurtures the soul.

—Rabbi Harold Kushner

28.

There is a law of gratitude, and it is . . . the natural principle that action and reaction are always equal and in opposite directions. The grateful outreaching of your mind in thankful praise to supreme intelligence is a liberation or expenditure of force. It cannot fail to reach that to which it is addressed, and the reaction is an instantaneous movement toward you.

—Wally Wattles

29.

Christians consider themselves not as satisfying some rigorous creditor, but as discharging a debt of gratitude.

—William Wilberforce

30.

Gratitude turns what we have into enough.

—Melody Beattie

Your Goals Will Grow You

Make a list of short-term goals you would like to achieve by the end of the year, month, or even week. As you accomplish your goals, give gratitude for the effort, inspiration, people, and other factors that helped you along the way. My goal is to see how I can give more to those around me, near and far. I would love to hear your aspirations!

Chapter Seven

July - Summer Is Love

As Far as Possible, Without Surrender, Be on Good Terms With all Persons

Let's Make it a Complaint-Free World

Go one day without complaining—even better, go a week. If this is hard for you to accomplish, it's time to make some changes in your life. Think positively, live in the present, and appreciate where you are and who you are. Today is a gift, accept and embrace it. Author Mark Bowen wrote a fantastic book on this very topic which I have turned to when I need a reminder, as all of us do now and again. My copy came with a bracelet, a simple way to monitor how often you complain, and helps you track your progress toward becoming "complaint-free." Put the bracelet on, and every time you complain, switch it to the other wrist. The goal is to go twenty-one consecutive days without complaining or switching wrists.. It is harder than you might think, and I was a bit shocked at what a complainer I turned out to be. It was a really good exercise for me and I highly recommend it. I benefited enormously and I suspect the people around me did, too!

1.

Thankfulness is the beginning of gratitude. Gratitude is the completion of thankfulness. Thankfulness may consist merely of words. Gratitude is shown in acts.

—David O. McKay

2.

None is more impoverished than the one who has no gratitude.

—Fred De Witt Van Amburgh

3.

Take full account of the excellences which you possess, and in gratitude remember how you would hanker after them, if you had them not.

—Marcus Aurelius

4.

We often take for granted the very things that most
deserve our gratitude.

—Cynthia Ozick

5.

Gratitude is a duty which ought to be paid, but which none
have a right to expect.

—Jean Jacques Rousseau

6.

When you change the way you look at things,
the things you look at change.

— Wayne Dyer

7.

Gratitude is the best attitude. There is not a more pleasing exercise of the mind than gratitude. It is accompanied with such an inward satisfaction that the duty is sufficiently rewarded by the performance.

—Joseph Addison

8.

Your attitude is like a box of crayons that color your world. Constantly color your picture gray, and your picture will always be bleak. Try adding some bright colors to the picture by including humor, and your picture begins to lighten up.

—Allen Klein

9.

I feel a very unusual sensation – if it is not indigestion, I think it must be gratitude.

—Benjamin Disraeli

10.

The gratitude of most men is but a secret desire of receiving greater benefits.

—Francois de La Rochefoucauld

11.

Thank you is the best prayer that anyone could say. I say that one a lot. Thank you expresses extreme gratitude, humility, understanding.

—Alice Walker

12.

At the age 18, I made up my mind to never have a bad day in my life. I dove into an endless sea of gratitude from which I've never emerged.

—Patch Adams

13.

On the recollection of so many great favours and
blessings, I now, with a high sense of gratitude,
presume to offer up my sincere thanks to the Almighty,
the Creator and Preserver.

—William Bartram

14.

I believe in prayer. I believe in gratitude
and serving people.

—Kiran Bedi

15.

When a person doesn't have gratitude, something is
missing in his or her humanity.

—Elie Wiesel

Yes, You Can

Remove the word "can't" from
your vocabulary and think about
what is actually holding you
back—fear, reluctance, pride?
Once you stop talking yourself
out of taking a risk or making a
difficult decision, life will open
up for you and so will your mind.

Do something nice and helpful
without being asked. Take out
the trash, clean the house, and
visit a relative. Once you make
a habit of these tasks, you won't
need reminding—you will want
to do them.

16.

To come to terms with our beginning requires a truthful story to acquire the skills to live in gratitude rather than resentment for the gift of life.

—Stanley Hauerwas

17.

Sometimes we should express our gratitude for the small and simple things like the scent of the rain, the taste of your favorite food, or the sound of a loved ones voice.

—Joseph B. Wirthlin

18.

Feeling gratitude isn't born in us – it's something we are taught, and in turn, we teach our children.

—Joyce Brothers

19.

Gratitude is a mark of a noble soul and a refined character. We like to be around those who are grateful.
—Joseph B.Wirthlin

20.

I have to read something positive every single day. I have to have faith that the day is unfolding in a way that is going to be useful to somebody else_ For me, living every day in gratitude has been profound for me.

—Lea Thompson

21.

Give yourself a gift of five minutes of contemplation in awe of everything you see around you. Go outside and turn your attention to the many miracles around you. This five minute a day regimen of appreciation and gratitude will help you to focus on your life in awe.
—Wayne Dyer

Recognize Excellence

Did you have a helpful or enthusiastic waiter at the last restaurant you went to? Call and tell the manager about the great experience you had. Did a coworker knock it out of the park during crunch time? Do you still think about a college professor that impacted you? Write them a letter to thank them. Many jobs are thankless jobs, so remember how good it feels to be thought of and appreciated, even years later. Also, telling your friends and family about your good experiences with these people can help their business flourish

22.

. I think, with never-ending gratitude, that the young women of today do not and can never know at what price their right to free speech and to speak at all in public has be earned.

—Lucy Stone

23.

Of all the characteristics needed for both a happy and morally decent life, none surpasses gratitude. Grateful people are happier, and grateful people are more morally decent.

—Dennis Prager

24.

If future generations are to remember us more with gratitude than sorrow, we must achieve more than just the miracles of technology. We must also leave them a glimpse of the world as it was created, not just as it looked when we got through with it.

—Lyndon B. Johnson

25.

Does not gratitude of the dog put to shame any man
who is ungrateful to his benefactors?

—Saint Basin

26.

Gratitude is the healthiest of all human emotions. The
more you express gratitude for what you have, the more
likely you will have even more to express gratitude for.

—Zig Zagler

27.

The simple act of saying 'thank you' is a demonstration
of gratitude in response to an experience that was
meaningful to a customer or citizen.

—Simon Mainwaring

28.

As with all commandments, gratitude is a description of a successful mode of living. The thankful heart opens our eyes to a multitude of blessings that continually surround us.

—James E.Faust

29.

We should honor mother earth with gratitude; otherwise our spirituality may become hypocritical.

—Radhanath Swami

30.

A man's indebtedness is not virtue; his repayment is. Virtue begins when he dedicates himself actively to the job of gratitude.

Desiderata
—Max Ehrmann, 1927

Go placidly amid the noise and haste, and remember what peace there may be in silence.

As far as possible, without surrender, be on good terms with all persons. Speak your truth quietly and clearly; and listen to others, even to the dull and ignorant; they too have their story. Avoid loud and aggressive persons; they are vexations to the spirit.

If you compare yourself with others, you may become vain or bitter, for always there will be greater and lesser persons than yourself. Enjoy your achievements as well as your plans. Keep interested in your own career, however humble; it is a real possession in the changing fortunes of time.

Exercise caution in your business affairs, for the world is full of

135

trickery. But let this not blind you to what virtue there is; many persons strive for high ideals, and everywhere life is full of heroism. Be yourself. Especially do not feign affection. Neither be cynical about love, for in the face of all aridity and disenchantment, it is as perennial as the grass.

Take kindly the counsel of the years, gracefully surrendering the things of youth. Nurture strength of spirit to shield you in sudden misfortune. But do not distress yourself with dark imaginings. Many fears are born of fatigue and loneliness.

Beyond a wholesome discipline, be gentle with yourself. You are a child of the universe, no less than the tress and the stars; you have a right to be here. And whether or not it is clear to you, no doubt the universe is unfolding as it should.

Therefore, be at peace with God, whatever you conceive Him to be. And whatever your labors and aspirations, in the noisy confusion of life, keep peace in your soul.

With all its sham, drudgery, and broken dreams, it is still a beautiful world.
Be cheerful. Strive to be happy.

I recently came across Desiderata and remembered how it immediately captured my attention long ago...in the 1960s. The words continue to hold true for me today as a clear instruction for Life.

Today's Practice: Desiderata

•Choose a line from today's reading that captured your attention.
•Make it your mantra for the day... and embody its' wisdom

Today's Power Statement: Your Desiderata Mantra

Use this as your mantra today

Chapter Eight

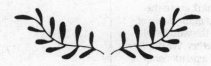

August – Life is Good!

As You Give, You Shall Receive

Catch People Doing Something Right (and Make Sure They Know It)

During difficult transitions, our natural tendency is often to contract and grow rigid. In this state we seem to only be able to focus on the negatives. We think about the despair and torment of the death of a loved one, but not the wonderful moments spent together. We think of the heartbreak of a relationship ending, but not of the exhilaration and freedom of being unattached. We might even scold our loved ones, or our friends, or coworkers for something minor or insignificant when we wallow in such negativity. But it is in these moments specifically that gratitude can be used to alter this way of thinking.

Finding positives and accentuating them is the easiest way to turn those proverbial frowns upside down and gray skies back to blue. Try catching someone doing something right for a change, not something wrong. Giving praise for a job well done lifts all parties involved, and is the easiest way to say, "Thank You," without actually having to say it.

1.

The discipline of gratitude is the explicit effort to acknowledge that all I am and have is given to me as a gift of love, a gift to be celebrated with joy.

—Henri J.M. Nouwen

2.

Fill the earth with your songs of gratitude.

—Charles Spurgeon

3.

Enjoy the little things, for one day you may look back and realize they were the big things.

—Robert Brault

4.

The way to develop the best that is in a person is by appreciation and encouragement.

—Charles Schwab

5.

Feeling grateful or appreciative of someone or something in your life actually attracts more of the things that you appreciate and value into your life.

—Northrup Christiane

6.

What you truly acknowledge truly is yours. Invite your heart to be grateful and your thank yous will be heard even when you don't use words.

—Pavithra Mehta

7.

In all affairs it's a healthy thing now and then to hang
a question mark on the things you have long
taken for granted.

—Bertrand Russell

8.

There is a calmness to a life lived in gratitude, a quiet joy.

—Ralph Blum

9.

Live your life so that the fear of death can never enter
your heart. When you arise in the morning, give thanks
for the morning light. Give thanks for your life and
strength. Give thanks for your food and for the joy of
living. And if perchance you see no reason for giving
thanks, rest assured the fault is in yourself.

—Tecumseh Shawnee Chief

10.

Find the good and praise it
—Alex Haley

11.

What if you gave someone a gift, and they neglected to thank you for it—would you be likely to give them another? Life is the same way. In order to attract more of the blessings that life has to offer, you must truly appreciate what you already have.

—Ralph Marston

12.

Having an attitude of gratitude lends a sense of satisfaction and generosity of spirit that will ease your way through the world.

—Brenda Knight

13.

I wanted to say thanks... and share my gratitude for everything I've been blessed with. Family, friends and continued support from everyone.

—Travis Barker

14.

Live with intention. Walk to the edge. Listen Hard. Practice wellness. Play with abandon. Laugh. Choose with no regret. Appreciate your friends. Continue to learn. Do what you love. Live as if this is all there is.

—Mary Anne Radmacher

15.

Gratitude opens the door to...the power, the wisdom, the creativity of the Universe. You open the door through gratitude.

—Deepak Chopra

As You Give, So You Shall Receive

I witnessed my mother tithe at church when I was a child and noted she did so with pride. I was also not unaware that she "did without," and did not get herself new purses or clothes or anything so she could take care of my sisters and me, and be able to give her little bit of extra pocket money to the church. I learned about self-sacrifice, and also about living from your values in this way. Experiment with tithing. There is a universal law of tenfold return. This means that when you give freely, your return is tenfold. You don't give to get the return; you give freely, and what you give flows back to you tenfold. Particularly in terms of money, many of us think the law of attraction doesn't apply. It does. Money is simply energy, and when you allow the energy of abundance to flow through you, money and other resources

continue to flow to you. When you stop the flow of abundance out of fear, anxiety, and worry, the flow of money stops. During the next six months, experiment. Whenever you get money, before you pay any bill, take 10 percent and give it to something you believe in. What is most important is that you give with an open heart.

16.

Make it a habit to tell people thank you to express your appreciation, sincerely and without the expectation of anything in return. Truly appreciate those around you, and you'll soon find many others around you. Truly appreciate life, and you'll find that you have more of it.

—Ralph Marston

17.

'Thank you power' is writing down the moments that are good in your life so that you can go back and reflect on them—so you've got this sort of repository of good stuff in your past.

—Deborah Norville

18.

We think we have to do something to be grateful or something has to be done in order for us to be grateful, when gratitude is a state of being.

—Iyanla Vanzant

19.

Saying 'thank you' creates love.

—Daphne Rose Kingma

20.

No longer forward nor behind
I look in hope and fear; but grateful take the good I find,
the best of now and here.

—John G. Whittier

21.

The best and most beautiful things in the world cannot
be seen or even touched—they must be
felt with the heart.

—Helen Keller

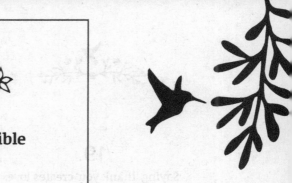

Mission Possible

Challenge yourself. Life is a process and during that process you should get to know yourself better, surprise yourself, and challenge yourself. If you go through life without trying something new, you are not doing yourself justice. Discover your true potential, and maybe more than just your life will be benefitted. Just step up and you'll be glad of it.

22.

Trade your expectation for appreciation and the world changes instantly.

—Tony Robbins

23.

There is no such thing as gratitude unexpressed. If it is unexpressed, it is plain, old-fashioned ingratitude.

—Robert Brault

24.

The struggle ends when the gratitude begins.

—Neale Donald Walsch

25.

. Gratitude is the single most important ingredient to
living a successful and fulfilled life.

—Jack Canfield

26.

Whatever our individual troubles and challenges may be,
it's important to pause every now and then to appreciate
all that we have, on every level.

—Shakti Gawain

27.

The aim of life is appreciation; there is no sense in not
appreciating things; and there is no sense in having
more of them if you have less appreciation of them.

—Gilbert K. Chesterton

28.

Gratitude is a currency that we can mint for ourselves,
and spend without fear of bankruptcy.

—Fred De Witt Van Amburgh

29.

Happiness is something that multiplies when it is divided.

—Paulo Coehlo

30.

We should certainly count our blessings, but we should
also make our blessings count.

—Neal A. Maxwell

Your Goals Will Grow You

Make a list of short-term goals you would like to achieve by the end of the year, month, or even week. As you accomplish your goals, give gratitude for the effort, inspiration, people, and other factors that helped you along the way. My goal is to see how I can give more to those around me, near and far. I would love to hear your aspirations!

Chapter Nine

September – Harvest Your Blessings

Pay It Forward as Far as You Can

Just Say Yes

I (re)learned this truly vital lesson from Imperfect Spirituality blogger and author Polly Campbell: once today say "yes" to something unexpected that comes into your life.

Know that you are enough to handle whatever emerges from the yes. Know that you have the whole Universe supporting you. Believe that you will have a good time and learn something that you need to know. Exercise your faith by taking the Universe up on the good things that come your way, and practice your optimism by believing that there is more to come. Just. Say. Yes.

Then take two minutes to reflect and answer these questions for yourself:

- What did you say "yes" to today?

- Were you inclined to first say "no"? Why?

- How did you feel when you said "yes"?

- What did you learn about yourself by saying "yes" to this thing?

- What do you know now that you didn't know before you took the leap?

1.

Gratitude also opens your eyes to the
limitless potential of the universe,
while dissatisfaction closes your eyes to it.

—Stephen Richards

2.

Reflect upon your present blessings, of which every man
has plenty; not on your past misfortunes,
of which all men have some.

—Charles Dickens

3.

Gratitude always comes into play; research shows that
people are happier if they are grateful for the positive
things in their lives, rather than worrying about what
might be missing.

—Dan Buettner

4.

Appreciation can change a day, even change a life. Your willingness to put it into words is all that is necessary.

—Margaret Cousins

5.

When you give and carry out acts of kindness, it's as though something inside your body responds and says, 'Yes, this is how I ought to feel.'

—Rabbi Harold Kushner

6.

Gratitude in advance is the most powerful creative force in the universe.

—Neale Donald Walsh

7.

Gratitude is a bridge to the heart reflecting
the beauty in our lives.

—Carol Adamski

8.

Before I get out of bed, I am saying thank you. I know how
important it is to be thankful.

—Al Jarreau

9.

Strive to find things to be thankful for, and just look for
the good in who you are.

—Bethany Hamilton

10.

I have a lot to be thankful for. I am healthy, happy and I am loved.

—Reba McEntire

11.

The trick is to be grateful for when your mood is high and graceful when it is low.

—Richard Carlson

12.

Let gratitude be the pillow upon which you kneel to say your nightly prayer. And let faith be the bridge you build to overcome evil and welcome good.

—Maya Angelou

13.

You pray in your distress and in your need; would that you might pray also in the fullness of your joy and in your days of abundance.

—Kahlil Gibran, The Prophet

14.

He is a wise man who does not grieve for the things which he has not, but rejoices for those which he has.

—Epictetus

15.

We can be thankful to a friend for a few acres or a little money; and yet for the freedom and command of the whole earth, and for the great benefits of our being, our life, health, and reason, we look upon ourselves as under no obligation.

—Marcus Annaeus Seneca

Learn the Art of Letting Go

After all, we are all human and we have a little baggage. Or a lot;I sometimes will hold in my feelings until it is like a dam about to overflow. Luckily for me, I have had the opportunity to learn from great authors like Sue Patton Thoele, Melody Beattie, and Mark Nepo that we just have to move on toward the positive. Release any repressed anger and pain that you have been harnessing. Allow yourself to let go of the past so that you can proceed to live in the present without worry, fear, or resentment. Remember that this isn't a one-time event, but a process. Letting go is an act of kindness for yourself and from yourself. Once you can accept that life isn't always something you can predict or control, yours will eventually become more positive and joyous.

16.

"I've learned that no matter what happens, or how bad
it seems today, life does go on,
and it will be better tomorrow."

—Maya Angelou

17.

As each day comes to us refreshed and anew, so does my
gratitude renew itself daily. The breaking of the sun over
the horizon is my grateful heart dawning
upon a blessed world.

—Adabella Radici

18.

The hardest arithmetic to master is that which enables
us to count our blessings.

—Eric Hoffer

19.

Gratefulness is the key to a happy life that we hold in our hands, because if we are not grateful, then no matter how much we have we will not be happy— because we will always want to have something else or something more.

—David Steindl-Rast

20.

Grow flowers of gratitude in the soil of prayer.

—Terri Guillemets

21.

The best way to pay for a lovely moment is to enjoy it.

—Richard Bach

Cartloads of Kindness

This one is so simple I really shouldn't have to write it here, but you'd be surprised how many people don't put their shopping carts away once they are done unloading their groceries. Walk the extra ten feet to the nearest shopping corral and roll that cart on in. Done! In addition, if you notice someone about to put their cart away and you need one, offer to take their shopping cart. These momentary connections that can happen in the frozen food aisle or parking lot are good for us. Keep us human. Keep us together.

22.

At the end of the day, let there be no excuses, no explanations, no regrets.

—Steve Maraboli

23.

When you arise in the morning, think of what a precious privilege it is to be alive—to breathe, to think, to enjoy, to love—then make that day count!

—Brenda Knight

24.

Appreciation is a wonderful thing. It makes what is excellent in others belong to us as well.

—Voltaire

25.

No duty is more urgent than that of returning thanks.

—James Allen

26.

Saying thank you is more than good manners.
It is good spirituality.

—Alfred Painter

27.

What matters most on your journey is how deeply
you see, how attentively you hear, how richly the
encounters are felt in your heart and soul.

—Phil Cousineau

28.

Giving is an expression of gratitude for our blessings.

—Laura Arrillaga-Andreessen

29.

I would rather be able to appreciate things I cannot have than to have things I am not able to appreciate.

—Elbert Hubbarb

30.

Let us learn to appreciate there will be times when the trees will be bare, and look forward to the time when we may pick the fruit.

—Peter Seller

31.

If you are not happy, act the happy man. Happiness will come later. If you are in despair, act as though you believe. Faith will come afterwards.

—Pico Iyer

Chapter Ten

October – Gratitude and Giving
Go Hand in Hand

Think "Best Case Scenario" All the Time

Pay It Forward

Stop for a moment and think of someone who needs a gesture of kindness. Perhaps it is something kind that someone once gave to you. With gratitude for what was given, reach out and give back. It can be a simple gesture, like sending a card, or calling someone who is sick and saying you care. You may well recall the movie based on the book, but if you want ideas and to connect to other kindly folks, go to www.payitforwardfoundation.org. Pay It Forward is about all people, from all walks of life, giving to someone else and making a positive difference. At last count, there were more than 500,000 people in sixty countries around the world participating on the day.

1.

Develop an attitude of gratitude, and give thanks for everything that happens to you, knowing that every step forward is a step toward achieving something bigger and better than your current situation.
—Brian Tracy

2.

The simple act of saying 'thank you' is a demonstration of gratitude in response to an experience that was meaningful to a customer or citizen.

—Simon Mainwaring

3.

All human beings are also dream beings. Dreaming ties all mankind together.

—Jack Kerouac

4.

I don't have to chase extraordinary moments to find happiness—it's right in front of me if I'm paying attention and practicing gratitude.

—Brene Brown

5.

It's a sign of mediocrity when you demonstrate gratitude with moderation.

—Roberto Benigni

6.

A man's indebtedness is not virtue; his repayment is. Virtue begins when he dedicates himself actively to the job of gratitude.

—Ruth Benedict

7.

Thanksgiving is a time of togetherness and gratitude.

—Nigel Hamilton

8.

Prayer becomes more meaningful as we counsel with the Lord in all of our doings, as we express heartfelt gratitude, and as we pray for others.

—Elder David A. Bednar

9.

Never lose childlike wonder. Show gratitude... Don't complain; just work harder... Never give up.

—Randy Pausch

10.

Revenge is profitable, gratitude is expensive.

—Edward Gibbon

11.

Thanks cost nothing.

—Creole Proverb

12.

When eating fruit, remember the one who planted it.

—Vietnamese Proverb

13.

**When you drink water, remember
the mountain spring.**

—Chinese Proverb

14.

**Social scientists have found that the fastest way to feel
happiness is to practice gratitude.**

—Chip Conley

Patience Is a Virtue Worth Cultivating

I love the old-fashioned ideas of virtues, such as kindness or generosity, a LOT. I am determined to develop my patience muscle so it gets stronger all the time. Here is a big one for me: to learn to have patience with difficult people. (And realize I may be one myself and not know it.) This is not only a good deed for the person you are exhibiting patience towards, but it is also a good deed for yourself. Imagine that, a good deed for yourself! For example, when someone is purposely trying to push your buttons by doing something or saying something rude, you can choose to act with patience and understanding instead of anger. This will benefit you by keeping your blood pressure low and your stress levels low as well—which we know are two health issues that many people are suffering from today. My wise woman friend BJ Gallagher says, "Difficult people are the ones we learn the most from."

15.

An attitude of gratitude brings great things; it is good
way to start each day.

—Mary Jane Ryan

16.

If you just feel happy for what you have...and be grateful,
then it will come true—you will be GREAT
and you will be FULL.

—Hugh Prather

17.

I begin every day by counting my blessings. Once you
have done that, you are ready for anything.

—Tony Burroughs

18.

Be happy for what God has given you. All happiness will come to you if you are happy. Happiness will come to you because happiness wants to go where happiness is.

—Allen Klein

19.

There is exactly one word in the whole dictionary which can represent God in you, which can bring knowledge in you, which can make you everything that you want to be, and that is 'gratitude.' This is an ecstasy, a bliss, an accomplishment, an achievement.
In English the word is 'thank you.'

—Yogi Bhajan

20.

To start with, you need to look at what you have and not at what you don't have. Without a sense of thankfulness, neither prosperity nor pleasure, joy nor happiness means anything. Mother Nature brings all the wealth, health, and happiness.

—Mary Beth Sammons

21.

If you just feel happy for what you have, no matter how simple, you'll be richer than any millionaire.

—Marc Allen

22.

This is the highest way of living, and is the biggest truth, the highest truth. You cannot live with applied consciousness until you understand that you have to be grateful for what you have. If you are grateful for what you have, then Mother Nature will give you more.

—Lee Ching

Charity is a Virtue

True generosity, with no strings
attached, expecting nothing in
return, and without scorekeeping,
is a direct expression of
abundance. Be generous
with your time and skills by
volunteering for something you
believe in; leave an extra tip for
the wait staff; give away thank
you's. Go through your closet
and gather up things you don't
wear or use, and donate them to
a homeless shelter or people in
need. Medieval scribe and exalted
thinker St. Augustine taught that,
"Charity is the virtue that brings
us closest to God."

23.

Love is love is love is love is love.

—Lin-Manual Miranda

24.

Be in gratitude. Make an attitude to be in gratitude, and you will find the whole Universe will come to you.

—Eileen Duhné

25.

Give to the givers, not to the takers.

—Clare Cooley

26.

Love is not enough; intelligence is not enough; powerful strength is not enough. You may put everything on one side of the scale, but if you are missing gratitude, you shall lose.

—Yogi Bhajan

27.

Appreciation is an art and a lifestyle and a source of happiness and fulfillment.

—Robert Leffler

28.

That mind which does not live in gratitude is just like a junkyard. There are great cars there, but they don't work; they are useless, because they are junk. What are you without gratitude?

—Louise Baxter Harmon

29.

The purpose is to be in gratitude forever. Live with applied consciousness, prosperity will break through the walls, flood you with it. You do prayer when you are in difficulty. Pray when you are not in difficulty! That is the art of thankfulness.

—Jay Kahn

30.

It is not that it is religious or it is not religious, it is called attitude of gratitude, it is called thanking God for giving you elbows and knees, giving you ribs and the glandular system, giving you head and skull and brain.

—Yogi Bhajan

31.

The ideal purpose of your life is that you are grateful—great and full—that you are alive, and you enjoy it.

—Nina Lesowitz

Think "Best Case Scenario" All the Time

Many people over-analyze situations, psych themselves out, and only consider the worst-case scenarios. I, for one, am guilty as charged. Let's start each day on a positive foot and make a list of your "best-case scenarios."

- What are the best things that could possibly happen to you?
- To your family?
- To your neighbors?
- To your coworkers?
- To the world?
- Have fun with this and think big!

Chapter Eleven

November – Count Your Blessings

Power Your Life With the Positive

Make Time for Gratitude Every Day

When we begin a daily practice of recognizing the positive events that occur and the pleasant encounters we have with others, we start noticing more things to be thankful as the days pass. Perhaps it's someone who holds the door for you at the supermarket, the nice conversation you have with a stranger while at the coffee shop, or a hug with someone you love. These are the small moments, and often the ones we forget. Savor their beauty and what they tell you about humankind—that we do live amongst many good people.

1.

A person who gives more than he receives
is absolutely divine.

—Sanskrit Proverb

2.

Gratefulness will make you great.

—Susyn Reeve

3.

What happens when you speak positive? When you
speak positive there is no negative left to express and
then there is a gap. Then in that gap comes the super-
positive and that's what we call God. It is an attitude of
gratitude. Attitude of gratitude is when you are grateful
for every breath of life.

—Yogi Bhajan

4.

Nothing is more honorable than a grateful heart.

—Seneca

5.

Feeling grateful or appreciative of someone or something
in your life actually attracts more of the things that you
appreciate and value into your life.

—Christiane Northrup

6.

Love wholeheartedly, be surprised, give thanks and
praise—then you will discover the fullness of your life.

—Brother David Steindl-Rast

7.

True thanksgiving means that we need to thank God for
what He has done for us, and not to tell Him what
we have done for Him.

—George R. Hendrick

8.

A thankful person is thankful under all circumstances. A
complaining soul complains even if he lives in paradise.

—Baha'u'llah

9.

God has two dwellings; one in heaven, and the other in
a meek and thankful heart.

—Izaak Walton

10.

What sunshine is to flowers, smiles are to humanity.
These are but trifles, to be sure; but, scattered along
life's pathway, the good they do is inconceivable.

—Joseph Addison

11.

The glory of friendship is not the outstretched hand, nor
the kindly smile, nor the joy of companionship; it is the
spiritual inspiration that comes to one when he discovers
that someone else believes in him and willing to trust him.

—Ralph Waldo Emerson

12.

A true friend is the greatest of all blessings, and that
which we take the least care of all to acquire.

—Francois de la Rochefoucauld

13.

True friendship multiplies the good in life and divides
its evils. Strive to have friends, for life without friends
is like life on a desert island. To find one real friend in a
lifetime is good fortune; to keep him is a blessing.

—Baltasar Gracian

14.

My father prayed because he had a good friend with
whom to share the problems of the day.

—Corrie Ten Boon

15.

I thank you for your kindness, I will not soon forget;

You're one of the nicest people I have ever met.

—Joanna Fuchs

Muchas Gracias

I learned from my globetrotting friend, Brad, that one of the nicest things a traveler can do is to learn how to say the basics in the language of the locals. He stressed that saying THANK YOU is the MOST important word of all. His guide to global gratitude is below:

Czech: Děkuji
Danish: Tak
Dutch: Dank u
Estonian: Tänan teid
Filipino: Salamat
Finnish: Kiitos
French: Merci
Gaelic: Go raibh maith agat
German: Danke
Hungarian: Köszönöm
Indonesian: Terima kasih
Italian: Grazie
Japanese: Arigato
Latvian: Paldies
Norwegian: Takk
Polish: Dziękuję
Portuguese: Obrigado
Romanian: Mulțumesc
Spanish: Gracias
Swahili: Asante
Swedish: Tack
Vietnamese: Cảm ơn bạn
Welsh: Diolch yn fawr

16.

But friendship is precious; not only in the shade, but in the sunshine of life, and thanks to a benevolent arrangement the greater part of life is sunshine.

—Thomas Jefferson

17.

It isn't the size of the gift that matters, but the size of the heart that gives it.

—Eileen Elias Freeman

18.

How can I find the shining word, the glowing phrase that tells all that your love has meant to me, all that your friendship spells? There is no word, no phrase for you on whom I so depend. All I can say to you is this, God bless you precious friend.

—Grace Noll Crowell

19.

Good news doesn't necessarily have to be a positive thing. Bringing good news is imparting hope to one's fellow man.

—Patti Smith

20.

The heart of the giver makes the gift dear and precious.

—Martin Luther

21.

I thank you, God, in Heaven, for friends.

—Margaret Elizabeth Sangster

Power Your Life With the Positive

When life gets you down, remember to look on the bright side (and there is always a bright side). Be strong not just for yourself but for those around you as well. Eleanor Roosevelt once said, "It is better to light a single candle than it is to curse the darkness." Look into the meaning of this quote: focus on the light in your life—and if there is none, try to be that light.

22.

One can never pay in gratitude; one can only pay 'in kind' somewhere else in life.

—Anne Morrow Lindbergh

23.

"Attitudes are contagious. Make yours worth catching."

—David Mezzapelle

24.

A noble person is mindful and thankful for the favors he receives from others.

—Buddha

25.

In life, one has a choice to take one of two paths: to
wait for some special day—or to celebrate
each special day.

—Rasheed Ogunlaru

26.

Cultivate the habit of being grateful for every good thing
that comes to you, and to give thanks continuously. And
because all things have contributed to your advancement,
you should include all things in your gratitude.

—Ralph Waldo Emerson

27.

The unthankful heart discovers no mercies; but the
thankful heart will find, in every hour,
some heavenly blessings.

—Henry Ward Beecher

28.

If you are really thankful, what do you do? You share.

—W. Clement Stone

29.

Look at everything as though you were seeing it for the
first or the last time, then your time on earth will
be filled with glory.

—Betty Smith

30.

Give thanks for a little and you will find a lot.

—Hansa Proverb

31.

The only people with whom you should try to get even
are those who have helped you.

—John E Southard

Chapter Twelve

December – Time for Celebration and Appreciation!

Life is a Kingdom, Love is the Key

Making Memories, Family Ties and Time

'Tis the season to... spend more time with those you love! Instead of spending time sequestered in separate rooms watching television, playing video games, or browsing the Internet, call all family members into the same room and do something together. Play a board game, watch a movie, have everyone contribute to making dinner, then roast marshmallows in the fireplace. Or maybe chestnuts. Do people really do that? Ho ho!

1.

The miracle of gratitude is that it shifts your perception
to such an extent that it changes the world you see.

—Dr. Robert Holden

2.

The root of joy is gratefulness.

—David Steindl-Rast

3.

Got no check books, got no banks. Still I'd like to express
my thanks—I got the sun in the morning
and the moon at night.

—Irving Berlin

4.

Act with kindness, but do not expect gratitude.

—Confucius

5.

Among the things you can give and still keep are your word, a smile, and a grateful heart.

—Zig Ziglar

6.

Gratitude is a quality similar to electricity: it must be produced and discharged and used up in order to exist at all.

—William Faulkner

7.

Gratitude is one of the sweet shortcuts to finding peace of mind and happiness inside. No matter what is going on outside of us, there's always something we could be grateful for.

—Barry Neil Kaufman

8.

The most fortunate are those who have a wonderful capacity to appreciate again and again, freshly and naively, the basic goods of life, with awe, pleasure, wonder, and even ecstasy.

—Abraham Maslow

9.

To speak gratitude is courteous and pleasant, to enact gratitude is generous and noble, but to live gratitude is to touch Heaven.

—Johannes A. Gaertner

10.

Integrate what you believe in every single area of your life. Take your heart to work and ask the most and best of everybody else, too.

—Meryl Streep

11.

Devote yourselves to prayer, being watchful and thankful.

—Bible

12.

The struggle ends when gratitude begins.

—Neale Donald Walsh

13.

If forgiveness is medicine, then gratitude is vitamins.

—Steve Maraboli

14.

Be thankful for what you have. Your life, no matter how bad you think it is, is someone else's fairytale.

—Wale Ayeni

15.

A moment of gratitude makes a difference in your attitude.

—Bruce Wilkinson

16.

The real gift of gratitude is that the more grateful you are, the more present you become.

—Robert Holden

17.

Gratitude is more of a compliment to yourself than someone else.

—Raheel Farooq

Forgiving and Giving

In Jewish literature, the sages have said that tzedakah is the highest of all commandments. In fact, it is equal to all other commandments combined. Tzedakah is what grants us forgiveness from our sins. According to the Yom Kippur literature, a judgment has been inscribed for those who have sinned. Repentance, prayer, and tzedakah can reverse the decree.

Certain kinds of tzedakah are considered to be of greater merit than others. Maimonides organized the different tzedakah into a hierarchical list. From the least to most meritorious they are:

- Giving begrudgingly.
- Giving less than you should, but giving cheerfully.
- Giving after being asked.
- Giving before being asked.
- Giving when you are unaware of the recipient's identity, but the recipient is aware of yours.
- Giving when you are aware of the recipient's identity, yet you remain anonymous.
- Giving when neither party is aware of the other's identity.
- Enabling the recipient to become self-reliant.
- Give, no matter what.

18.

Don't pray when it rains if you don't pray when the sun shines.

—Leroy Paige

19.

Nothing new can come into your life unless you are grateful for what you already have.

—Michael Bernard

20.

I am grateful for the blessings of wealth, but it hasn't changed who I am. My feet are still on the ground. I'm just wearing better shoes.

—Oprah Winfrey

21.

If you want the rainbow you have to put up
with the rain.

—Dolly Parton

22.

When you give appreciation in order to get something its
manipulation and people can sense it.
Appreciate genuinely.

—Marilyn Suttle

23.

Let gratitude be the pillow upon which you kneel to
say your nightly prayer. And let faith be the bridge you
build to overcome evil and welcome good.

—Maya Angelou

Season's Greetings

As your family arrives—or as you arrive at your family's—to celebrate Christmas, greet everyone with a genuine smile and embrace. Leave any past disagreements or arguments at the door and see the good in everyone. You love these people and they love you. Bond over happy memories and the amazing dinner spread on the table. In our family, we always invite people who might not have anywhere else to go. I well remember being new in town in San Francisco and an "orphan" with nowhere else to go on the holidays, and kind people took me in. That meant so much to me and still does, so I remember the kindness and pass it on at Thanksgiving and the Christmas holidays.

24.

As a child, I didn't know what I didn't have. I'm
thankful for the challenges early on in my life because
now I have a perspective on the world
and kind of know what's important.

—America Ferrera

25.

Forget yesterday—it has already forgotten you. Don't
sweat tomorrow—you haven't even met. Instead, open
your eyes and your heart to a truly precious gift—today.

—Steve Maraboli

26.

When we give cheerfully and accept gratefully,
everyone is blessed.

—Maya Angelou

27.

When all seems lost, stop where you are and think of three things you are grateful for. You will feel much better immediately. Make this a morning prayer.

—**Becca Anderson**

28.

Gratitude is the state of mind of thankfulness. As it is cultivated, we experience an increase in our 'sympathetic joy,' our happiness at another's happiness. Just as in the cultivation of compassion, we may feel the pain of others, so we may begin to feel their joy as well.
And it doesn't stop there.

—**Stephen Levine**

29.

Wake at dawn with a winged heart and give thanks for another day of loving.

—**Kahlil Gibran**

30.

You've got to be one that, wherever you are, like a flower, you've got to blossom where you're planted. You cannot eliminate darkness. You cannot banish it by cursing darkness. The only way to get rid of darkness is light and to be the light yourself.

—Cory Booker

31.

When you give and carry out acts of kindness, it's as though something inside your body responds and says, 'Yes, this is how I ought to feel.'

—Rabbi Harold Kushner

Parting Wisdom

Enough is abundance to the wise.
—**Euripides**

Gratitude and attitude are not
challenges; they are choices.
—**Robert Braathe**

Gratitude doesn't changes the
scenery. It merely washes the
clean the glass you look through
so you can clearly see the color.
—**Richelle E. Goodrich**

No one who achieves success
does so without acknowledging
the help of others. The wise and
confident acknowledge this help
with gratitude.
—**Alfred Northhead**

After Words

Be Grateful For Each Other, Be Grateful Together
by Brenda Knight

In closing, we thought we would share with you one last way that you can express all of this newfound gratitude, and that is by opening up a "Gratitude Circle." The idea is simple. A gratitude circle is a place for sharing stories, photos, prayers of gratitude, and videos with friends and loved ones. The more people you can get to align with you, the sooner you will discover the positive power of gratitude and reap the many benefits that come from doing so. Now, we want to spread that gift and help you become cheerleaders for others who have tapped into the power of thankfulness by forming your own Gratitude Circle.

By creating a Gratitude Circle, you can join us in being grateful. Connect with others in this special group that's dedicated to honoring the simple phrases, "Thank you" and "I am grateful for...." We know firsthand that once you start a thankfulness circle, it won't take long

221

for others to join in, and the power of gratefulness will permeate and bless your everyday being.

There are several ways you can take part in a Gratitude Circle—you can create your own Gratitude Group. We make it easy for you with our tips for starting a circle.

Opening to Thankfulness

1. As the organizer of the Gratitude Circle, consider yourself the host or hostess, almost as if you have invited a group of friends—or people you hope to become friends—to your dinner table. Your role is to help guide conversations and serve up a feast (of interesting stories about gratitude or nuggets of information to share) that will keep the conversations meaningful, inspiring, and ultimately bring to life the power of gratitude in all the lives of those gathered in your circle.

2. Create a Mission or Goals for your Gratitude Circle. What do you want to accomplish? How will you manifest gratitude in your own life and the lives of those in your circle? Will you share stories, inspiring quotes, guided meditations? Create a plan for guiding your group through the practice of gratitude.

3. Decide Whether to Meet Online or In Person. The exciting thing about the Internet is that you can create a Gratitude Circle and community online and connect friends and colleagues from across the country—and the world. Or you may want tocreate an in-person circle with friends in your neighborhood or town.

4. Send out evites, invites, and make phone calls to invite members to your Gratitude Circle. Ask everyone to invite a friend and spread the word about your new group.

5. Select a meet-up place. Often guides will invite in-person communities to meet at their home. Or you may opt for a local coffee shop or a comfortable meeting place where you can gather regularly.

6. Create a calendar of meet-up dates and distribute to your group.

7. Create Gratitude Circle materials. In this book we have lots of prompts for discussions about gratitude and thankfulness. Please feel free to tap into these as resources.

8. Spread the good news about what being thankful can do as it manifests in your life and the life of your friends, family, and members of your Gratitude Circle.

Circles of Grace

Those simple suggestions should help you and your Gratitude Circle get started. Remember, nothing is cast in stone, and you can feel free to improvise until you find your comfort zone. We guarantee you will come away from these gatherings feeling inspired, challenged, and with exciting new ideas to share.

First, begin by welcoming your guests. Go around the circle, each person introducing themselves. For example, "I am Mary Smith and I live in Ohio. I am a writer, literacy volunteer, and mother of two." Next, read a passage of poetry, prayer, or prose.

We recommend sections of either the Introduction or the beginning of Chapter Two of this workbook. Now, go clockwise around the circle, and ask each participant why she or he is here and what spiritual sustenance he or she is seeking.

Ask a volunteer to read her favorite prayer or quote about being thankful.

These group gatherings are wonderful, but personal sharing and goal discussion can be intimidating at first, so be mindful of your group and you'll sense when you will need to wrap things up. Always end on a high note by asking each person to share gratitude. May your transformation be your inspiration!

Epilogue

Love Is the Key

Well, you've been weeping and wailing and
complaining a lot.
It seems like all you ever talk about is what you ain't got.
You're never gonna make it,
Don't you know that it's true?
Until you get in touch with what's inside of you.

You've got all makin's of heaven on earth.
You've had it all right there inside you since the day of
your birth
You got the brains to think,
The eyes to see,
You got the heart to love,
You've got the will to be free.
Life is a kingdom, love is the key.
All you gotta do is just let it be.

Life is a song,
Life is a dance,
All you gotta do is just take a chance.
The Buddha, Buddha, the Buddha he knew

The Buddha, the Buddha, the Buddha's in you.

Well the world is so wide and there's so much to do,
There isn't much time for being lonely and blue.
So pack up your sorrows, swallow your pride;
Your tank is overflowing, let's go for a ride. You can
build for tomorrow if you live for today
But all the fear you borrow just gets in your way.

Life is a river,
So get in the flow,
Dance to the rhythm,
Let yourself go.

Well. You got billions of years of history,
It's all written in your body,
In your chemistry. When you learn to reach in,
Then you learn to reach out,
That's when you reach the answer to what life is about.

Just like the story of the prodigal son,
We're all working our way back to where we begun.
And when we get there, we will have what is true
And we will love it so much better because of all we
been though.
Life is a kingdom, love is the key.
All you gotta do is just let it be.

Life is a song,
Life is a dance,
All you gotta do is just take a chance.
The Buddha, the Buddha, the Buddha, he knew
The Buddha, the Buddha, the Buddha's in you.

—by **Peter Krug**